Making Pizza

Written by Sarah O'Neil
Photography by Michael Curtain

sundance

Ingredients

pizza crust

tomato sauce

cheese

green peppers

salami

olives

Get the tomato sauce and the pizza crust.

Put the tomato sauce on the pizza crust.

Get the cheese.

Put the cheese on the pizza.

7

Get the salami.

Put the salami
on the pizza.

Get the olives.

Put the olives
on the pizza.

Get the green peppers.

Put the green peppers on the pizza.

Put the pizza in the oven.

Now it's done.

Try some—yum, yum!